Wolf Trees

Wolf Trees

POEMS

BY
Katie Hartsock

ABLE MUSE PRESS

Able Muse Press

www.ablemusepress.com

Printed in the United States of America

Library of Congress Cataloging-in-Publication Data

Names: Hartsock, Katie, author.
Title: Wolf trees : poems / by Katie Hartsock.
Description: San Jose, CA : Able Muse Press, 2023.
Identifiers: LCCN 2022027875 (print) | LCCN 2022027876 (ebook) | ISBN 9781773491202 (paperback) | ISBN 9781773491219 (ebook)
Subjects: LCGFT: Poetry.
Classification: LCC PS3608.A78756 W65 2023 (print) | LCC PS3608.A78756 (ebook) | DDC 811/.6--dc23
LC record available at https://lccn.loc.gov/2022027875
LC ebook record available at https://lccn.loc.gov/2022027876

Cover image: *Daydream* by James Dexter Havens

Cover & book design by Alexander Pepple

Able Muse Press is an imprint of *Able Muse: A Review of Poetry, Prose & Art*—at www.ablemuse.com

Able Muse Press
467 Saratoga Avenue #602
San Jose, CA 95129

To Jonathan

Why wait any longer for the world to begin?

Acknowledgments

I am grateful to the editors of the following journals, where these poems originally appeared, sometimes in earlier versions:

32 Poems: "Appearances and Realities"

Able Muse: "Eye Cup"

Beloit Poetry Journal: "Marriage Bed with Medical Devices" and "Needle in a Haystack"

Birmingham Poetry Review: "Wolf Trees," "Wolf Tree beneath the Gown," "Where the Wolf Tree Nurses," and "The Wolf Tree in Film"

Dappled Things: "John Wayne Brings Wyatt Earp a Cup of Coffee"

Ecotone: "Coywolf"

Flyway: Journal of Writing & Environment: "Grotto"

The Greensboro Review: "The Busted Maraca"

Grist: "If you secretly wish your child could be secretly baptized," and "The making of a mullet"

Image: "And it came to pass in those days"

Iron Horse Literary Review: "Glucose Tablets"

Jesus the Imagination: "Wolverine" and "Child with Droid"

The Kenyon Review: "The Nipple Shield of Achilles"

Mezzo Cammin: "Studies in Devotion"

Missouri Review: "Tree Wolf"

Nimrod: "Trying,"

Pericles at Play: "The Rash" and "Musculature"

Pleiades: "A Paraklausithyron"

Poetry: "Breast Milk"

The Raintown Review: "The Watercolorist"

Southern Indiana Review: "In Decent Seas"

The Threepenny Review: "Negative"

Trinity House Review: "Flashes in All Directions" and "The mother's stomach, a kind of tree"

What Rough Beast: "On His Beauty"

I want to thank my family and friends who give my poems their warp and weft, especially these amazing women: my mother, Mary Ann Hartsock; T. Hetzel, Jessica Wright, Darci Cooper Whitman, Francesca Tataranni, Helen Polowy, Amelia Jarret, and Ruth Martin Curry; and Mary Swartz and Barbara Hartsock, my wolf tree grandmothers in the heavens. I want to thank my friends and colleagues who gave invaluable support for and feedback on these poems: Susan McCarty, Alison Powell, Annie Gilson, and Dunya Mikhail. Endless thanks to my forever-mentors Jim Cummins, Lorna Goodison, Linda Gregerson, Laura Kasischke, Mary Kinzie, Reginald Gibbons, and Marianne Hopman. Thank you, Alex Pepple, for supporting my work, and for everything you do for contemporary poetry. I also want to thank all the poets of an annual December writing group, led by Laura Passin, where many of these poems began to take shape.

Thanks to my brother and my father, David and Dave Hartsock; and to my parents-in-law, Deborah and David Geltner (who was the first person I ever heard say, "That's a wolf tree.") I want to especially thank the family of James Dexter Havens: Anne Havens, and Abby Letcher, who gave permission to use his 1934 woodcut *Daydream* as cover art. Finally, I want to thank my husband, Jonathan Geltner, and our sons, Harlan and Arthur Geltner, for the heart and light they shine every day.

Wolf Trees

Was once common to compose a poem to stay the saw: *Spare,
woodman, spare the beechen tree* . . .
    — C. D. Wright, *Casting Deep Shade*

This new technology has turned me into a cyborg. But not the
human-machine hybrids rhapsodized about by futurists and
able-bodied biohackers. . . . Most cyborgs are not superhumans
approaching a postbiological future, but rather people with
disabilities trying to live a normal life.
    — Stu Sherman, from introduction to
      Living With: Self-Portrait of a Diabetic Life

. . . he shot up like a sapling, I nurtured him like a tree on an
orchard slope . . .
    — Thetis, *The Iliad*

Wolf Trees

i.

Breast Milk

The eyes wide or weighty
with it. The full boat
or low tide of it.
The leopard of it
when it leaps. Nervous
before a sermon, Saint Bernard
prayed for help and the Virgin appeared,
babe in lap, to squirt him in the eye
with a wondrous stream of it,
thus gifting him with eloquence.
The sun-white glow of it
in dimmed-down rooms
across galaxies, galaxies, galaxies.
The Romans admired a mother
who visited her father, sentenced
to starve to death, in prison,
and kept him alive with it,
secretly. The leopard
of it when it leaps.
Ten children my great-grandmother
nursed, from one breast—
the other side never made, maybe,
a country doctor thought,
because of her childhood polio.
The creation *ex nihilo* of it,
across the galaxy's pale cream.
In a short story by Maupassant,
a train is stopped far from anywhere

and one car holds two strangers,
a very hungry man and a nursemaid,
painfully engorged. And that's all
you really need to know,
except, it occurs to me, she
must have been hungry too.

Wolf Tree beneath the Gown

For months she couldn't travel.
Now she's driven the hours and minutes,
she's entered the hospital lobby

where pictures of her hometown park
are blown up as wallpaper:
she's seen the silver bridge

that's magic to cross, the limestone boulders
where she's climbed giddy into their smells,
and the immense riverside tree,

a local favorite, with a bifurcated trunk
split by such a smooth scoop people
sit and pose there. It's always reminded her

despite herself of legs spread high in the air,
despite herself of a woman's legs,
and despite despites

that tree has stirred her,
walking beside a Frank or a Luke on the path.
She's ridden the elevator, she's marked

the room numbers closing in, and now they are crying,
she and her mother, each telling the other,
everything's all right now.

Her mother needs more care
than she's ever seen her need.
When the aide comes in to clean her up,

the mother turns on her side,
facing her daughter. Her gown falls open
and the daughter looks.

The surprise calms her. All this
and so pretty, the hair
and skin and shapeliness.

Negative

*To whoever crossed out with a blue X the word "Sea" written in
white cursive on the top iron guardrail of my second-favorite bridge
over the Huron River*

Of course it's not.
Were you angry, were
you sad? Are you
a disgruntled former employee
of the earth? You
have company. I know
some walks can get
you nowhere. I've seen
one child take away
a toy from another
not because they wanted
the lamb or train
or drum, but they
saw the other kid
so happy with it.
And a "no" erupts,
a need to negate
what might be someone's
favorite thing. When I
first saw what you
did, I yelled across
the water, startling swans
with their bottoms up
through air and beaks
deep in dioxane-plumed mud

back to the surface.
Their hearts can't say
what's been done to
them either. And why
did you use such
a pastel Marian shade
of blue? Why does
your X have that
strange sense of elegance,
patience, uncannily equal to
the word it came
to cancel? Almost as
if it were you
who first wrote "Sea,"
in a burst of
jubilant heresy, a fit
of twenty-first century Duchampian
reverence, a mood where
the world could be
different, when water itself
could be baptized, revised.
Then came a day
terribly certain that no
better difference is coming.
A day to recant,
not erase, your work.
A day like today.
I feel it too.

Marriage Bed with Medical Devices

I kept saying no to sticking you on
my skin, to computer chips between
him and me, vibrating the nightstand

with alarms. When I did fill out the forms,
when I augmented,
we drove to the other side of the great lake

and there in the rush of its body I felt you,
little barnacle, on my thigh,
and you, bee-eyed satellite

of my stomach, and sunlit cold water streamed
over you as over me,
thus convinced I still was mine.

And his. He'd say *Oh sorry*
at first when he touched or bumped
you along the usual routes.

By now, if you are not my true topography,
then what? You know how I can be
lying down like lake water wanting parted

by a swimmer's surest strokes, like an idle
power button waits to be pressed, to turn on
its perfectly working world.

Studies in Devotion

He reaches for my insulin pump, the size
of a strawberry under my sleeve. He thinks it's me,

the programmed opaque reservoir that feeds
my blood in drips. Expecting it to yield
like skin to his touch, he outlines the hard edges
until enough is known, for now. We shift
into the pose of mother and slippery child

in Raphael's *Madonna di Foligno*,
the painting a doctor prescribed to me. Not for

Jerome or his lion, not for Francis's hands
like winter branches singing to faraway shapes,
not for John the Baptist, his Rod Stewart hair

and wiry biceps, and not for the woman
or the babe who squirms to sail out of her arms;
my doctor—she was very good—directed
my gaze to the children's faces surrounding Mary.

They have become the clouds they float inside:
some look at her and some look at each other,
some have been reading James Wright and cup
their sister's cheeks. *They ripple tensely, they
can hardly contain their happiness. . . .* Others

prefer Leonard Cohen. *They are leaning out
for love and they will lean that way forever.*
Look at them for a long time a little each day,
my doctor instructed, and I did, holding

a screen in my lap in a Chicago flat. The man
who commissioned the work kneels below them, caped
in fur-lined red. Something fiery fell from the sky

and into his house, but he lived. *Paint me alone
among the saints, paint me in my gratitude.*

This happened years ago. On earth they gather
around the ground torn open by the disaster,
a womb of nothingness that filled, healed shut,
and now these green and yellow tufts grow there,
as if dormant seeds were harrowed back to life.

And in the middle, across his messenger's chest,
a cherub holds a blank bronze plaque, still waiting
for its words, the way the uninscribed can wait.

Eye Cup

*An Ancient Greek drinking vessel with a face, usually with
prominent eyes, underneath*

Draining it, you lift a mask:
a satyr, a monster, a brighter-eyed man

painted on the bottom of your kylix.
The foot of its stem is the cartoonish

nose, and its handles, rounded ears
you finger-grip so you can wear

your new face. And everyone laughs
as you shoulder-sway, drink the last

few drops, let some dribble down your neck
from a head not quite connected.

The streak runs red and then pale red.
But I know you. I know you best

in the early sips, when the cup's eyes just cover
your mouth, you look at me with four

ways of looking, and someone else
who's also you drifts in the lees.

Coywolf

Some creatures hate you seeing them.
They lean into a wind away
with faces full of spleen.
When the coywolf came to me, her eyes

said, I have not come to you at all,
and then a second thing, some
beautifully put imperative—
I have forgotten it—to forget

coywolf, which I have not
completely. It was a summer evening
when the coywolf came to me;
sphinx moths snorted lavender juice

in landscaped prairie weeds along the lake,
the great lake that glows like dawn
as it goes dark. I stood
by a maritime pitch pine, the needles

I like to touch. Like one memory you keep,
and no others, of a lover who said
Come here my flower and pulled
you onto him—like touching a memory

like that, that's how to hold its needles.
The lake lapped at the shoreline,
one wave regurgitated itself
into the cavernous riprap

and I turned to the dull bell of sound,
to where the coywolf sat—
poised like a dog told to sit,
nearly chameleonic with her concrete-

gray fur, her stillness of a building
against breakwater stones.
Have you ever eyed your enemy
and thought, *No Never Not if we were the last*

two people on the planet—the coywolf comes
from getting over that.
Come here my flower. When the coywolf came
to me I could not stop looking

in her eyes, as she let me, if I kept consenting
to be forgotten, as I did.
Their mission has no mission, no hidden hybrid
agenda, except to live. So coywolf learns

the lapdogs' schedules, the last pee
of the night. Coywolf knows
how many bones wait in the rack of ribs
you brought to the barbecue, can tell

by your baby's inhalations
if she's about to laugh or cry.
Coywolf sees you with your frozen fish
and all you have to do is thaw it, in water

that falls right out of your faucet.
Coywolf knows you have an errand
and you think it will be quick,
no need to latch the back screen door.

When I found the coywolf come to me
and she said, you have found nothing
and never will, it was dusk;
as I stood searching like a human

the night bloomed into blackness
beyond the sidewalk lamps—
I saw it. And I left.
I think about the coywolf as indistinctly

as I can: asleep on her bed of reddened needles,
or dangling from her maw a squirrel
limp as a long-traveled letter
that promises good news, but not for us.

The Wolf Tree in Film

From her car seat a child saw a cow
in a field and touched her window
as if it were a smartphone screen,
moving her thumb and forefinger
to enlarge the figure. Some images
become our own. I was born

beneath a wolf tree. You've seen wolf trees
in all the movies—casting
shade for lovers or a villain's fried chicken
lunch spread on gingham cloth,
and the treasure buried beneath its roots.
A tree that is the forest that is
the island. A tree like a street

named Forest I liked to walk toward
at sunset, where the line
of trees behind the houses looked
so much more distant than
they really were. A tree to lean
against and think, I'm there.

Trying,

as it's called. Even after losses, still trying.
Climbing through woodland dunes,
even still I could hold an aspen leaf to my ear,
let it dangle and ask, What do you think?
When I saw the eyeless head and the legs in shreds
on a baby turtle, shell intact, even still
I made a bier of sticks, balanced the body there,
set it down inside the dune grass and lightly
buried it. Even still the old poem
where a baby god is born and crawls
out of his mother's faraway cave, and sweet-talks
(in full sentences) a mountain tortoise
into coming inside so he can
slit her throat and scoop her out and string
her shell with sheep gut string and begin
to sing of his own conception, of his own
glorious birth just a minute ago—and thus
he invents the lyre—is dear to me.
                        I wanted
to write my miscarriages but I had to keep walking
into them so we drove around the great lake
to stare at it from different lots, logs, cliffside
benches with gold-plaque inscriptions and dates,
little elegies with lines like "Jeez-oh-pizza!":
a favorite phrase of one friend of the forest.
And I had to watch TV and eat.
Even now I'll still search YouTube for the best montage
of Julio and Alicia's kisses and my grief

comes back to me, fricative like their youth
and beauty, the subtitles of their Catalan tongues.
A-lee-thee-a. Hermes was a god of many things,
of thieves and dogs that do not bark
as thieves complete their work. The baby hid
his lyre then set out to steal Apollo's cattle,
herding them backward so it looked like they walked
right up to the very spot where they should have been
and just evaporated.

      I spoke to our lost ones
often and every day of each month
I bled again I would get lit then go dark
for the night. The wine-dark sea was me.
Even still I bought a teal green miniskirt
and taught in it. Even still I looked at old albums
with my father's mother and there she was
posing like a pinup against gravestones:
she'd slipped over the cemetery fence
with the other girls on break from nursing school
to take the sultriest pictures and I felt
the power. Papa looked over and whistled,
and even the faded mermaid on his forearm,
tattooed in navy blue, who no longer danced
when he flexed his wrist, perked up a little.

           Naturally
the two gods feuded and only their father and music
could settle it. Hermes gave Apollo the lyre
and then they were brothers, sons
who bowed their heads together to the prayer
of bottom lips bitten down on: *If I could say one word*
to change the world against your will,

I would not speak. How classic is that.
Boston came on the radio and even still I sang loud
alone in the car and called it karaoke to my Lord.
I kissed my husband's hand and undressed
that gesture of submission. We would come home late
as Hermes did the day he was born,
slipping like a mist through the keyhole.
Even still his mother took him in her arms, the liar
swaddled in his lying, the terrifying tiny bully
who wanted his godhead but even more a family
and just had to get their attention.
                              Even still I miss
my mother's mother's house, how on holidays
we'd repeatedly, inscrutably, cram all our bodies
into her entryway, way too small to hold our hellos
and goodbyes but it did, somehow; we hugged even
as we held casserole dishes warm and heavy
or cold leftovers, still a little heavy.

In Decent Seas

I used to walk Chicago's harbors, emptied every winter,
and every winter I would miss the names of boats.

At certain times of day pigeons fly in overlapping
helices, dotting the i's on the names of their boats.

Ancient sailors were farmers, plowing the surly gray.
The sea's fencing and furrows sang the names of boats

before anyone wrote them, or painted their letters blue
with pastes of indigo leaves and herbs with names like boats.

Think of a desire turned into a satisfaction turned into a joy
turned into a joke. That's how to name your boat.

It's me and not me when Tom Petty sings the name Katie
in "About to Give Out." Which would be a bad name for a boat.

Grotto

He took the woman who'd handed him gym towels
to the back of Beaver Creek State Park's tall grass.
Let's make a little cyborg. How many alcohol
swabs have I torn and touched like a cool mustache
to my skin, with its infusion sites, red marks
of crayoned hearts tilted, medicinally.
Tonight I measure insulin, press start,
and hear my body beep. All its batteries

are ready. And if the world runs out it will be
a slow decline. I came from a grotto created
by the bodies of a man who would always need
more and a woman who could do any job she could get
so well that soon nobody did it better than her
until something would happen and it would be over.

Needle in a Haystack

It's something people say
as an excuse to stop searching.
They forget that I still go

to the barn, ready to catch
the slightest glint of a silver line.
The day it fell away,

I held its eye up to mine
and finessed a thread to stream straight through,
as sunlight did in the hayloft wall,

the shadowed wood so pinned
with beetle holes, I saw a starry night
from where I sat. It dropped

and made no sound except
a dread of dropping, echoed in
each thing I found, digging down:

a chessboard's cobalt castle,
a fountain pen that wrote in cursive
hay-streaks through my hair,

a vine with red blossoms
the stack's own sediments had sewn.
To clapboards, swallows, mice,

I prayed with Latinate
datives: *bring it me, bring
it me.* The walls engraved

themselves in calyxes
and spirals, and I would wake with earwigs
at my neck and knees and elbows.

I watched hydrangea petals
petrify come autumn, rustle
like hungry dogs in the wind

where hunger turns mean things
sweet. I will walk with you, as promised.
I have some pleasantries

to exchange, my gaze trained
on earth's colors as they shift,
ready for invention.

ii.

Wolf Trees

i.

I cut down a forest and left one tree.
I put to pasture the berry-eyed beasts
who could lie with horse flies in its shade.

And I spread its acorned branches
outward and upward into what
would be a telltale shape, a crown

without hindrance, a Vitruvian Man
risen out of the ground at his groin
and stretching all of his arms to their fullest

circumferences. I changed my mind—
let the farms fail and trees swarm
back over the land, a forest again.

I watched saplings try to find
a way up around the oak, a behemoth
over all the new growth, a mouth

continuing to drink its accustomed jugs
of sun and rain, a gnarled bouquet.
I called it a wolf tree.

Katie's going wolfing again, my mother would say. A phrase she picked up from a romance novel she reads every summer, set in frontier days out West. A young woman apparently falls in passionate love with the brother-in-law she meets once she and her husband, who's really an awfully nice guy, start homesteading. To cover his, of course, gambling debts, the brother-in-law, another good man but with a, duh, grizzly demeanor only she, duh, can soften, goes hunting for wolves, to sell their pelts. It's desperate, dangerous, not very lucrative work, and he heads out alone. *Don't go wolfing*, she begs every time. What will she do. *Katie's been out wolfing*, I'd hear when I'd do crazy things. A little worried or wistful, she used to say it.

iii.

Bring me the broad-chested earth.
A wolf tree in the forest stands a remnant

of the field where it spread high and wide,
the field where it stood a remnant of

a razed forest. Wolf trees, perhaps,
because when the forest came back, they preyed

on the growth of new timber, in a forester's logic
where prohibitive becomes predatory.

Or, because they should be, like wolves, eradicated,
as the early twentieth century manuals advised.

Avaricious flora. Unfit
for life. But some say a wolf

because the trees stand alone, looming above
new diminutive woods,

apart from their packs that fell
to long-ago axes, apart

from the old familial milky scents. And somewhere
I read the suggestion, a wolf

owing to the size of these trees, which cast
such shadows where wolves can hide.

iv.

When I was diagnosed with Type 1 diabetes I was twenty-six years old and my first thought was *Do I have to stop drinking beer.* When I was twenty and mugged at gunpoint on a 2 a.m. front porch of a sloping Cincinnati street I said to the half-masked man demanding my purse, *Let me get my cigarettes.*

When I was diagnosed I did not know my body, grown thin, had been starving. I thought I looked fantastic, even in my exceptional thirst and exhaustion. Diabetes, from the ancient Greek for *sieve,* because untreated it does not let you process nutrients, you just piss everything out. Hence thirst as a telltale symptom.

A disease of great antiquity: when I peed on holy cliffs over the Aegean or flood plains by the fertile Nile thousands of years ago, doctors noted the bees and ants that flocked to the puddle. One took a sample to taste my flushed out sugars. Hence the name *diabetes mellitus.* A sieve, a sweet one.

The first diabetic in the United States to receive a new drug from Toronto was James D. Havens, the future woodcut artist. It was 1922 and he was twenty-two and about to die. But in blood, doctors had found the right islands (*insula* in Latin, hence insulin) to extract and inject, mimicking a pancreas. Havens's Wikipedia entry shows him holding one of his children and describes his body of work as trying to *depict the dynamic, but often unseen, processes of nature.*

Being a good diabetic is lonely work. I stand in the middle of a field, I stand in the middle of the forest watching others eat and run and cook and walk down all the well-stocked shining aisles and never check their numbers. The numbers change so fast. Sometimes I see another silhouette like mine, chiseling its life into the sky, one more day. I see its reaching branches. I know the reach without touch.

A century ago, I'd never have got to the age I am now. Decades ago, my body would have been sternly advised against bearing my sons. A wolf tree in a pasture or forest or suburban street where New Englanders or Midwesterners or Pacific-Coasters use the term—in Britain they say legacy trees, or veteran trees—looks around and thinks *What do they mean, a wolf. And why do I recognize nothing from my youth. And why was I not cut down like the rest.*

v.

Some tree surgeons call dead limbs wolf branches
and saw them off.

When I was thirty-two I looked at an ultrasound screen and saw
a black-and-white still life

where weeks before the same scene had pulsed with a heartbeat
in a miraculously strange ballet.

A nurse I'd never met held the wreck of me in her bosom
as broad as the broad-chested earth;

I let her and I loved her and I hated her. She was so clearly
a mother.

Because it was a Friday afternoon I had to wait until Monday
for the scheduled dilation and curettage

that would remove what one doctor called the materials. I walked
the weekend away,

my body the sandaled grave of our first child. Staring at Lake Michigan
from the city's riprap shore,

we smoked cigarettes neither of us tried to stop the other
from buying, after we'd mostly quit

for so long. Hence my cough that Monday, before
the twilight anesthesia.

34

vi.

My mother plays "Clap for the Wolfman" on any jukebox that's got it. She goes to powwows every chance she has, to see the dancers in their regalia, to eat frybread and succotash, to hear the drums, to revere the flags, to stand during the Grand Entry as if in another country. In that Guess Who song—*I said you're what I've been dreamin' of / She said I don't want to know*—the singer drives around with a girl who stays put to keep listening to Wolfman Jack, the cat on the radio who joins in the song—*Oh, you thought she was digging you but she was digging me*—with his jive talk that made so many young Americans suspect there was more going on, much more, than they'd been led to believe.

These powwows, she says, are big with the vets. The emcee lists the names of nations represented, ending with veterans. And many of this tribe are present. Honor there for warriors, Native and non-Native alike. Recognition of histories that often go without. She claps when the song claps, the same way she did in John McCartney's car. *It all depends on how your boogaloo situation stands, you understand.* John McCartney went and came home never the same and everyone was wrong to think the two of them would marry. Most dances are not for the public—the Snake, the Buffalo, the veterans' dance—but when the intertribal round begins she enters the circle, joins hands, and stomps the earth in time with strangers.

Once someone brought what they said was a wolf on a leash, would not let anyone pet it. There was, she says, no love in its eyes. At the vendors' tables, there're lots of skulls for sale. Spirit animal tapestries, bears and eagles and wolves, of course, in flannel or velvet. Lots of motorcycles and Mexican blankets. And other skeletal matter. From the top of a glass case she picked up a smooth small stick and was told with a laugh it was a petrified raccoon's penis. *If you've got the curves baby I've got the angles.*

vii.

The author of the 1945 essay "Woodman, Spare That 'Wolf' Tree!" was once a boy who adored a bluebird's nest every time he climbed his favorite oak. One day he found a black snake on its branch and the blue mother squawking at the stomach that bulged with the solar systems of her blue eggs. He tried to strike the snake, missed, fell, spent weeks with his arm in a sling. Later he'd argue against the protocol to cull these giants. Later, he'd say it's death and decay that lets the forest live. Later he'd list the scores of animals that make wolf trees their home, and note the wood duck, about whose ducklings naturalists since the time of Linnaeus have disagreed on how they get down from such high roosts into water. *Some say the mother transports them through the air on her back or in her bill. Others say she pushes them out of the nest and they drift as gently as a down feather. . . . There are other versions, too, which may or may not be verified.*

viii.

You're a little long in the tooth to be having a baby, my grandmother chuckled at me. Wolf trees don't have teeth anymore. In fact, their gummy open gullets are more like wombs. The sparrows know something like this—they who built a nest in the growling mouth of the dragon statue down the street, flying freely in and out.

She grew up in the Depression and usually does not laugh at her own jokes. Like a wolf tree, her face is the craggiest kind of beautiful. *An old diabetic*, she'd call herself, with some bitterness. She is not many years away from becoming a snag, a decayed and hollow trunk all the conservation biologists are now likewise advising, *Don't cut down!* Precisely because they're dead, they shelter life.

I don't think she was being mean. I think she likes saying things other people don't. To preserve certain turns of phrase— *long in the tooth* or *I won't have no truck with* so-and-so. I think she was worried. Head nurse of the maternity ward for decades, she once delivered ten babies in one night. Once, a fifteen-pound baby. *The mother was an old diabetic*, she said, laying every ounce of blame on the body she had seen inside. And the baby? *Not good to look at.* I think for all her worries she likes the spirit of a good surprise, like her remark once that Sean Connery probably has plenty of good sperm left. Another virtue of the wolf tree—in their old age and breadth, they are prolific seed producers.

Or like a watermelon roast—hearing that I attended a bonfire on a beach with a group of friends, she asked if we had a watermelon roast. *What's that?* Oh, it's when guys and girls have a fire, and someone throws a watermelon in, and it explodes, and everybody goes into the bushes and has a piece.

ix.

I pressed my cheek to the bark of a wolf
and sang "The Very Thought of You."

I read *Sons and Lovers* and remembered what it was
to wander far enough back in the forest
to find a place where no one would see.

I looked up once and a buck was watching us
against our waist-high fallen trunk.

His face showed such
recognition. Oh, they
do this too. So much that's recognizable

will not be known again.
Or new. The last time I arrived

at the bench in the back of the woods,
where I can follow
the lay of certain skinny trails even when they're covered

in autumn, where some things become invisible, things like
Southern Boulevard or the backyards of housing developments

or the loading docks of Best Buy, I saw
the words carved in timbered hammered beams,
I knew some of the hands

that had knifed or keyed them there, and I sat
on them, I sat beside them, I who did not need to rest.

x.

I'm a lone wolf, my brother would declare in his Wicca days. Not part of any pack or coven. Once he brought home a tiny broom from the Shaker Woods Festival, where one can buy the quaint kitschy crafts of a people named after the ecstatic spasms suffered while speaking in tongues. He intended to sweep away evil spirits with its bristles, so miniature he held the whole length of the broom in his hand. Our mother looked at him. *Don't worry*, he said, *I'm not going to ride around on it.*

My husband tells me that if he were a single man without children he would live in a small town in Tasmania. Other places don't appeal so much, New Zealand, etc., etc.—he catalogs the islands he's considered for this other life. So much nonsense about islands, when the likes of Muriel Rukeyser and John Donne have already solved it. *They're all connected underneath . . . No man is . . . I think I'd go to Ireland*, I say, already drifting. But that's a lie. I know exactly where I'd go.

xi.

In the days I drove long distances alone
in a '99 Cougar named Purple Haze,
I opened the moonroof whenever the weather allowed

the sky to become less separate. I looked for the trees
that stood apart in fields, turning my head
as from a barstool to trail their silhouettes,

as if they were the ones passing me by. As if
they'd know me, as if they too had been wanting
a recognition scene with someone, something,

they'd never met. And all this was before
the onset of the disease, before the disease
set itself on me. Before I'd heard anyone say,

that's a wolf tree. Her limbs are loveliest
at dusk, reaching her reach the daylight made
into the shy seductions of nightfall,

or so it looks to me when the air gets flushed,
deeply flushed with blue, with changing light
and the urge to create and touch, and withdraw and hide

then touch again. I can feel the path or sidewalk
get lacy with these shadowed moods. When I stretch
my arm out of sleep to check my CGM,

or quiet its high or low alarms, or pick up
my PDM to tweak the stream of insulin
dripping from a canula clicked down

beneath my skin, sometimes I keep my eyes closed,
my hand combing like a mole the nightstand
for the right robot in my robot stack I keep

close by. Sometimes I reach the other way
with eyes still shut to find my husband's shoulder
or neck or trunk or hand. How can I touch

without waking, how can I say without
speaking what he could understand as he sleeps,
how can I filter into him as a wolf tree

once talked to me. I was thirty-six. It was just
after dark, on one of my pregnant walks
I would take to lower my blood sugar for the baby,

the baby, the baby. And I'd have thoughts. *I wasn't
meant to be doing this*, or, *We shouldn't be here.*
At the wolf tree's edge, I stood beside another

whose blood remains, its engines louder because
remnant. Her body a body that owes some favors.
I touched her bark and felt a jolt, I held on

and felt the hush. The quickest sweep of headlights
pulling in a driveway made us shine.
It was one of those nights when the new moon's up there
somewhere, and I knew where.

iii.

John Wayne Brings Wyatt Earp a Cup of Coffee

Before he became John Ford's leading man,
the Duke worked for him in props and got
to meet the Tombstone marshal,
the ancient and real cowboy

who had come to teach tanned actors all his ways
of being real—how to walk while carrying a gun,
how to fall down whenever hit with a bullet.

I wouldn't have guessed they could have met,
these different centuries of men
and Wests. As when an older Ovid, on his way

to exile, might have met a teenage Christ
at some crossroads of the empire,
and the epic erotic tragic elegiac poet

locked eyes with the youth in a way
that made the sagebrush whir
and thrum below the signposts
to that big sky country, wild at the borders.

If you secretly wish your child could be secretly baptized,

I know someone. She was the girl who would forget
her mantilla for the weekday Masses, so the nuns
bobby-pinned an ivory Kleenex to her head.

In the days when all the bridesmaids had to go confess
after the rehearsal, she went drunk. The priest
called her by her first name right through the screen and asked
"Have you been drinking?" She doesn't believe in confession.

She drives on unpaved roads to country shrines to pray.
She did not get a cell phone until the summer of 2017.

She has been to a crucifixion: in a party town
on Lake Erie in the seventies she watched a group
of young men high on many things in the a.m. hours
nail the wrists and ankles of their friend to the wall
of a gift shop on the strip. She watched them take him down.

She has helped push over a barn that needed burning. She
is one of Hallmark's most enduring customers.
She quick-cleans her bathroom and says, "I gave it a kiss and a promise."

She has seen angels and, at a powwow near Ashtabula,
a vision of Janis in a drum circle, raising
her hand to shout-sing, "Someday!" She prefers the Nicene
to the Apostles' Creed. She will warn you about the speed trap

on Fairground Boulevard. She says, "I curse my heat,"
and shakes her fist at the sky. And then she looks at the sky.

She says, "This would have never flown in the seventies." She says,
"I look like a bad night in Girard." She says, entering
a room of people texting people beyond or even in
the room: "Sounds of silence." The first time she saw her daughter
smoke a cigarette, she ripped it out of her mouth,

tossed it in the extra tall bin of the Irish bar and started
singing Sting: "Then you'll find your servant is your master."
She has memorized reported words of John the Baptist—

"Isn't he sexy," she'll say, "with his camel hair
and all that honey"—and she'll recite them right into your eyes:
"I baptize with water, but one far mightier than I
is coming, whose sandals I'm not worthy to untie,

and he will baptize with *fire*." I tell you this
so you can understand your potential celebrant,

who will wait for a moment alone. She knows the formula,
she does not ask permission or forgiveness. She'll dip
her fingers in a water glass, or lacking that,
spit in her hand, and take your child to the river.
We all have excuses. I found one to leave the room

where she rocked my son, in the blue hour of the innocent.

Flashes in All Directions

Who is responsible
for the terrible times I've laughed—
when someone else's child

fell from a chair at my table, when I learned
about the faultless boy Life-Flighted off the football field
or what nuclear fission

can do? When I parked
by a wood I'd never walked before
and I saw the fence binding

its twenty acres, and its unlocked turnstiles—one entry,
one exit—radiating bars eight feet high,
and its rows of barbwire

above the fencing, tilted in—not to keep any climbers out
of, but to keep them inside,
this FENCED NATURE AREA,

as the signage read—I laughed and pushed my way in.
The pearlescent light of a low winter sun getting lower
made the chain-link glint

and trees stood spray-painted with the usual
suspects of hearts, PEACE, a penis, initials, pluses.
One trunk said, I SEE YOU,

a forest spirit turned panopticon, like the fiery sword
that flashes in all directions
outside the garden needing guarded since the day

God went for a walk in his woods
and found a man and a woman trying to hide
everything, and asked them

my favorite question God ever asked:
"Who told you that you were naked?"
It always makes me laugh.

Musculature

That's beautiful, my endo said,
examining my graph
of glucose levels on a day
I never went above

one-forty, or below eighty-five:
a more or less straight line
in a report which often reminds
us diabetics, and

our doctors, of a roller coaster
with hills and dips of high
and low blood sugars. But this horizon
was my sculpture, made

intently as a tricky drive
where many turns are missed,
made intensely as love with one
you will not see again,

in a body that would have perished years
ago, if not for the invention
of artificial insulin.
Arte factus, "made

with skill." If I could reproduce
such minimalist lines
every day, I'd never die.
Call it curated. Call

it radical. Call its excess
Whitmanian, this blood
sugar of mine, that loafs at its ease
and sometimes in largesse.

I saw a colossal statue once,
the Farnese Hercules,
and stood eye level to his quads.
He held behind his back

the apple he tricked his way into winning,
like I trick my way into living.
It's all a little Sisyphean.
His apple must return

to the garden; always I'm measuring
another dose, hoping
it's right, just as my pancreas
would do if it could again—

an enchanted tree welcoming home
a plucked-off piece of fruit,
regrowing the stem into its branch
so even the sepals shone

golden as an evening nymph.
I heard our hired guide,
a Ray-Banned Neapolitan,
explain the hero's muscles

are so exaggerated here
he couldn't walk if he came
alive; his body wouldn't work
one labor, lift a feather,

would just collapse into a pile
of useless hunkitude.
What if my touch, autoimmune,
could whittle him human:

file down biceps, inflate the hip furrows,
flat as a prophet envisioned
the world: *Every valley shall be
filled in, every mountain*

and hill made low. As if we would
be good, all good, remade
to live smooth as that landscape, where
I'd never want to walk.

Covid's Metamorphoses

I know—I know, sorry! Sorry. It's this basement
desk, this heavy rain, that has me thinking of
that wet poem, book one's great flood, the threat made good.

The first bodies to change in Ovid are cosmic,
the sky in love with earth so the horizon is just
a fuck-line, and then men and women and then,

as a crab says to a mermaid in the song my toddler
lately wants on repeat, "Ariel, . . . The human world,
it's a mess." Ergo, a dry decision to start again.

I know the boys are upstairs destroying a train track
they haven't finishing building, I know my husband's T-shirt
shows an Imperial AT-AT Walker falling

to its knees at the Battle of Hoth, with *FAIL* in all caps:
the walking tank's last robotic thought, perhaps,
in one of many moments we thought the resistance could win.

And the rain has slowed. When the world is drowning in Ovid,
the waters rise so high dolphins swim through trees,
sleek tips of dorsal fins grazed by the highest limbs.

In their eyes, so much mortality and so much brain,
so well aware of its limits, of what's bearable.

The mother's stomach, a kind of tree

that grew with such an unchecked reach it looks
like a wolf about to leap, on prey or pups
ventured from the den too soon. Each branch a crux
becoming other crosses, knots, nooks, bulges
of elbow ache, or pilonidal clefts.
Its bark still wants to stretch toward every claw
or wing or mandible that left its nests
and its limbs paunchy all year with autumn.
And when it lies on its side in bed, what a face
it makes! When she breathes, it breathes too. Of those
who loved this body when it was uncut paper,
she thinks of you. Of some scenario:
your torso back with hers, nervous to move.
You fill your hands and call it beautiful.

The Rash

Like a criminal it had its reasons
and eluded understanding
for far too long. Antibiotics, and a dairy

and soy intolerance, made the baby's stool
so frequent and acidic it burned his flesh
just the same as flames would have burned.

The doctor used words like *corrosive* and *caustic*.
Bent over him weeping I thought we made
a scene somehow left out of *The Inferno*:

the man whose midlife crisis knocked him down
to hell's own gastric acid, and his guide—
a poet from two thousand Roman years

ago, whose tomb Italian teenagers still
get arrested for breaking into, to get it on—
descend a hill tapestried with fire

to a field like a blistered hide, where hiss
the bile ponds and their runoff streams of scum
that excoriate whatever they touch. Now

they see me, wilted over the changing table
at the mouth of my fountainless cave, my grief
a record skipping beneath its needle:

as soon as I get a new diaper on, the child shits
and shrieks again. And clear-complexioned goblins
see to it that my diaper stash and all the stuff

I marshal to protect his skin—Maalox, Calmoseptine,
aloe vera, and Vaseline, topped with cornstarch—
remain eternally replenished. Dante asks,

"Oh, mother with your bird's nest hair and crooked
back, what have you done to earn your place
in these . . ." And then he still talks for a while.

They wait for my reply, the red depths
of my monologue. While they watch me fold
the diaper, the wickedly necessary diaper,

I speak, briefly, about tenderness.

A paraklausithyron

is an old kind of poem
addressed to the door
of a house you want to get into,
where someone you are into
lives. Evening sees you return

to that door that stays shut,
and if it would only open wide enough
your song could change from lament
to love. Our campaign was long
the season I canvassed a city

and its hinterlands, ostensibly
for John Kerry. At the time it felt dire,
that nothing could be more
important, and I knocked on doors
from hefty moneyed houses

that gave me lemonade in clean tall glasses
to the most falling-down
places. And by no means,
we were told, could we ever enter,
anywhere. About to ring

a bell on a dead-end street, I saw
through a picture window a naked man
asleep on his couch, and on top of him
a crested iguana the length of a golf club,
also sleeping. Sitting together

on the cool concrete of her front steps,
I wept with an old woman
who had just buried her son
and finished her story, *but yes but yes
I'm voting for Kerry.*

In a Mill Creek Valley housing project
I can't find now on a map,
no one on my Palm Pilot's list
of registered names
came to the door; everyone said

of everyone, *They don't live here
anymore.* Laundry hung from windows
to dry in the air that smelled
like a leak of something
nobody should breathe.

Standing in the dirt courtyard,
I looked up and could see, high
on the highest hill, my university,
where I'd taken in so many times
the almost panoramic view,

and I never knew.
Once a man who lived on a State Street
tried to get me inside,
behind his door, with him.
But that's not how the poem goes.

Predicated on separation,
stubbornness, and never-having,
the paraklausithyron,
and always ending with another plea.
I walked through an America about to vote

and it made me dizzy sometimes,
how I could smell some intricate history
at each threshold—bread baked,
a pet gerbil, a toxic cleaner or clingy cologne,
the rubber of a tricycle's handlebars

and the plastic of its streamers,
an ashtray between two tumblers
left behind the night before.
I was often sure someone was home,
who would not come to me for anything.

Wolf Trees of the Cross

Don't cut them down.
And keep the worlds that keep them uncut.

On the Dingle peninsula, they grow in a winding line
up the face of Mount Brandon, pockmarked with them.
Like Bill Murray's cheeks.
And just as irresistible, wise.
Hazarding a bet on outrageous love.

I made the climb in boots I hated.
Up the stony ascent steep with sheep shit.
I'd stop to catch my breath and read
from a Wikipedia page pulled up on my phone.
The sentences of what happened at each station.

I was out of shape with grief.
And the ocean and the mountain
as deep as my shapelessness.

He and I were nearing the top when we saw a young woman
near the bottom, starting up alone.
I wanted to stay at the summit for hours.
The clouds fast-moving around my body,
inched up to the edge and belly-clung to it.
And the paternoster lakes a thousand feet below.
As ready for prayer as anything.

The young woman arrived in strappy sandals I couldn't believe.
And I've got it in me to believe.
We left before she did but she passed us
on the way down, which I took slowly.
I too had stumbled for a second time at the seventh station.
I swore and sat for a while beside its sawn trunk.

On the same path medieval pilgrims walked.
Centuries before deforestation.
When we got to our car the girl was leaning against hers.
Smoking a cigarette.

That night we met a Veronica at the Courthouse Pub.
The roof hung right over our heads.
Like a stranger you want to let get close.
The session played, and the Guinness.
I told her, we climbed Brandon today.
She said I'm Veronica, I'm the one
who wiped his face at number six.
You never know what people will say.

What they will think of your climbing the stations.
When Francesca and I came down from Monte San Constanzo
I told the man who sold us limoncello
and wheels of provolone I would smuggle home
wrapped in dirty underwear to put off the customs dogs at O'Hare
we had just walked up that ridge of crosses.
"Oh did you do that?"
And he smiled like you smile at something outdated.
Or when you will immediately forget what a child just said or did.

But nothing can cancel what a child just did.
She and I had climbed through cypress groves
that told a story we couldn't really remember.

As we rose the vista widened:
Vesuvius, the Bay of Naples, Capri.
And other islands given perfect island names.
Like Ischia. With its towns like Stomach and Eyelid.
And other parts of the blazing monster and would-be rebel
the marbled powers kept caged below.

You and I might call him Typheus but the Italians call him Tyfeo.
Because some names just sound better in other languages.
Because some sons just want to rip the ground open
and get back to us.

Or at us. She and I sat, leaning on the white wall
of a windowless church.
Its door locked at the top of the mountain.
Eating strawberries and talking into strong wind.
In a place like that.

At the end of the trail
of steel Roman numerals
nested in bare boughs to trill, *Still here.*
Still here. Don't cut them down.
And keep the worlds that keep them uncut.

Appearances and Realities

Like when the rock
of the mango finally ripens
and I slice off its cheeks,
score its flesh, scoop half out
to one son and half to the other;
then I carve away chunks
from the pit, dividing this
second round as I did
the first; then I nibble away
whatever's left, and to the boys
it looks like I'm enjoying
the biggest fattest piece,
like I'd saved it for myself.
And they protest, and want some.

But really I'm gnawing a bone.
But really I'm scraping bits
with my teeth like a slate-beaked
parrot who knows a lot of words
she's taught herself not to say.
But really I'm chewing a stone
I stepped on long ago,
walking into the water
of an island's hill-licked bay.
I went in wearing summer
clothes, I could not not go in—
staring at my feet on a bed
of rocks who were round and bright
with as many colors' mercies
as any kind of fruit, who were
so glad I was there.

iv.

The Busted Maraca

And what made the music spilled all
over, myriad grains of glass beads,
so many colors, I wondered why

when by design they should have never
been seen. The bright intestines shook
in their sparagmos, gamboling

like spirits, like celebrities.
A scene like my own autopsy
interpreted as an action painting

gone off the canvas, the room
was a party and its aftermath
at once. I gathered what I could.

I will find them for years: paper lanterns
caught in branches, dwarf planets
rediscovered, flecks of ash

from another country's eruption blown
into a woman's hair going gray
to light it red then disappear.

To Dervla Murphy's Mother, in a Time of Quarantine

An invalid for thirty years,
bookended by piles of pages
you couldn't turn, concerned with tasks
beyond your reach, like islands

of dust on curtain lace—*castaway,*
castaway—you got mean.
Who wouldn't, when the dream where you
can't move won't end, when no door

leads outside. What house is built
for that. My mother's feet
surprise me when I cut her toenails.
She still walks but not that far,

hasn't traveled much and yet she'll say,
"Let's go, I know what walls
look like." On bumpy roads I push
a stroller built with shocks,

suspension, real wheels we keep inflated.
No Alterrain Pro
or Revolution Flex 2.0
for you, who pushed your pram

up into the Knockmealdown Mountains
on walks alone with the baby,
the year that would be your last to walk.
It was talked about.

It wasn't done: a mother taking off
to wildflowers, vistas,
ridges, freshest unbound air.
But you did. And when you died

Dervla rode her bike to India.
She stayed inside with you
so long, until you could wander
again, so far, with her.

Glucose Tablets

They taste like chalk might, sweetened: slow like thought
to crumble, but quick to disappear, absorb.

Starting insulin, I started waiting
to screw up my body's new mathematics;

I remember the first low blood sugar like any
first time. The room, the rug slightly spinning.

It was true, what Lorene had said: that it would feel
like frantic pedaling, on a bike with its chains

come loose, until it was over. Words are terrible
whenever I chew glucose tablets, flying

in and out like swallows here and gone
from nests improbably bird-spit-glued to the top

floor eaves of the Brutalist-style library
where I sat watching them, not writing. A poet

visiting campus once told us, Writing poems
is not so hard. He saw the blackboard's silver

tray and said, I'll do it now. He spoke
in line breaks of his first-grade teacher, the chalk

dust smeared over her clothes, the just-wet smell,
the petrichor, of erasers he would clean after class

piercing his boyhood's nostrils like a drug before drugs,
the maternal and the sexual, the White Cliffs

of Dover, far across the sea and in his hands.
That's all it is, he said, chewily.

You see something and think of something else.
Let the remembering begin, and end.

And it came to pass in those days

*that there went out a decree from Caesar Augustus, that all the
world should be taxed. And this taxing was first made when
Cyrenius was governor of Syria.*

— Luke 2:1–7, King James Version

I hear these words in your voice no matter who says them, in
the well-water smell of the basement, by the artificial tree you
and she would one day put a sheet over, so you never had to
take it down or put it up again. Its tall white bulk waiting in
the corner bothered me. I was older then. In the beginning
I was with my cousins, some loved and some unknown, at
your feet while you read the red-ribboned page from Luke,
and my uncles, some loved and some unknown, stood around
drinking in the background, making lewd gestures David and
I would recognize much later, watching home videos with
your ashes on the mantel. I didn't get to grieve you; you died
days after my first miscarriage. And I didn't come home. Last
night in the hour of midnight Mass I opened the curtains, and
streetlights and high oaks and five inches of new snow filled
the room with a glow like bulbs underground as I rocked my
firstborn. Whose head the sunrise flooded this morning, with
its unsparing horizontal beams, in such a wave I cradled a corona
as I nursed him, golden headed, I am telling you. You whom
I can talk to when I hear those names, Caesar Augustus and
Cyrenius, governor of Syria, to which the province of Judaea
had been added for a census.

Child with Droid

There's a heartbeat in you
whose mother blow-dries her hair
by the stalls while you sit
a white towel spread
between the locker room bench
and your nakedness perfectly
cloaked by your posture

as in a masterful painting
masterful centuries ago
a putto but a girl
this time and holding the phone
she gave to divert
you who cannot use it

Staring it down absolutely intent
you are uninterruptable
as *Boy with Thorn* the sculpture
I photographed with a disposable
camera how belovable
his concentration on
plucking that spine from his foot

And so the familiar impulse of mine
to pick you up is halted
not by the familiar prohibition—
Katie you cannot just
pick up other people's children—

but rather as by the museum signs
I kept reading one summer
Berühren verboten   *Non*
toccare   an outstretched
hand in a red circle
with a red line through it

You pay as little mind
as that boy beautiful of course
beautifully hunched over
in absorption like yours
and reproduced so many times
from Hellenistic fountains
to the Esquiline hill
to Medici gardens even
Napoleon confiscated a copy

And Brunelleschi when tasked
with *The Sacrifice of Isaac*
gave one of the servants
who abide with the ass
at the bottom of the mountain that same boy's
position of distraction

He never looks up to check
what manner of worship
works his master
but only attends
to that thorn in his arch

Who chose that Genesis scene
for the open competition to ornament
the Florentine baptistery
Who wanted parents coming through the doors
with babes in arms to see
that close call

Brunelleschi's piece
took second place
and was not used it is thought
he paid too much attention
to the servants' bodies
diverting the eye
from the main quatrefoil
the knife the angel the halted arm
Here I am says Abraham

Your mother is coming
her hair is dry but you
still stare at the blank dark screen
you cannot dig it out

The making of a mullet

never thought
I would, but
I get it
now I've let
it happen—
a stamen
his curls nursed,
an outburst,
a gold brick-
work helix,
a world we
set loose—he
never lost
the lowest
swell of hair
I revered
from the first—
the deep earth's
deepest root
proven true—
but just too
long now, so
I am told—
I have held
the scissors,
have acquired
a locket—
I can't cut it

Tree Wolf

I think there's something wrong with me. I'm pregnant, it's summer, and summer bothers me. This bothers me. The zoo's new Wolf Wilderness sits on two acres. The wolves must hear, not far to the south, the depressed highway pouring itself out in eight lanes. It is bothered, too. I saw the wolf near closing time. She was panting in the stupid humid afternoon, she had climbed into the lowest branches of a pine tree, which she was using to scratch her stomach. She was looking around, finding her acreage insufficient. I wanted to bring her a bowl of ice water as I would a dog. Watch her eyebrows rise, surprised at the cold. Not that she would. Domesticated dogs evolved this capacity to make us love them more. That she can't do this does not bother the wolf. Fuck raising my eyebrows for love. I've been smothered in AC this summer, I can't get comfortable without it, and when I'm comfortable I'm bothered. The comfort is killing us. The sound of a staple gun kept puncturing the air, rhythmically working on an exhibit for animals the wolf will never see. She'll hear them, she'll smell them, she'll taste their smell and sound. Everyone got used to it, forgot it was even a noise. But not the wolf.

The Watercolorist

It happened on an island, somewhere on earth.
What to do when a species goes unextinct?
We swore a hard pact never to say a word,

thinking of tranquilizers, cages, the blink
of power lines dissecting the wide-eyed air,
networking hinterland whose lonely instincts

rolled the stone away from the shore's sepulcher.
Why do you seek the living among the dead?
an angel asked women expecting a corpse.

We checked encyclopedias, old sketches
of their sepia face and form, to make sure,
and their Latin name, scrawled in elegiac lead,

flickered. The watercolorist was the first
to see them. Napping at the edge of landscape,
where trees' full bodies face the sun, uncovered

as close skin and procreative smiles laid
out on a nude beach, she heard the forest floor,
its stages of decomposition where they played

and did not cease their play when they noticed her.
After a few more sightings, one touched her toes
resting on rocks as she dozed, but that never

happened again. They let us watch them, almost,
it seemed, putting on a show of shining limbs
that could move the afternoon. Like being stoned,

the novelist said; or, the librarian
added, falling in love. Or like whatever
makes you feel God, said the chef, pouring Chinon

as we described what it was to be near
them. We knew we weren't any good at it, and
that when we left we'd never see each other

or them again—if we dreamt of the island
at the same time, maybe then. But who am I
and why should I break our pact here? Son of man,

sit on your ass and I will speak with you, I
can cover my tracks, I live three continents
away, always, wherever you are, I write

through some poet sequestered in Michigan
so the creatures are safe. An earth can remake
earth but slowly, acting up in subtle hints.

It's not as if I could slap your face and say,
I'm the goddamned mother goddess, little turd,
and you'd care. Or see, renewed, the light of day.

Wolverine

Lord I love your trees. I've loved them early, on
walks to lower my blood sugar before
I nurse the baby with this broken body given
me, which can live in the time you gave me form

and blood, this time on earth that gives us robots
full of math and insulin. I call the little one
Elf, my helper. Lord when the sky looks hard enough to drop
and break, I will love your trees, stunned

but not surprised by rain. I know your clouds
from above, too, because we fly in planes
in this time you gave me. Lord I am stumbling, bowed
with a beer in the backyard as the dusk spreads its bouquets

within your trees, dark as the Iron Age.

Lord I love the lights in the front yard
of a house just one block north of us, yellow
globes of light. Prismated, with a solar-
powered look. If my husband walked through their glow

right now, right through the glowing space they make
between houses, I would recognize his shoulders
and his gait, the contours of his face,
his clean-shaven jaw or even-trimmed beard.

My two husbands, I call him who changes
and stays. Thanks to change, maybe, we stay.
Years ago, after I'd said yes, we kept on talking. Marriage,
we thought, is like a sonnet—the content craves

the form, which must mean more than fixity
and innovate like a leaf. Lord I love your trees.

The Nipple Shield of Achilles

When Thetis mourns her son before he is dead, she says, *I raised him like a tree in a sloping orchard.* Or, maybe, *I nourished him like a tree*—or, *fattened, cherished, gave strength to, gave suck to.* I had a terrible time when I started nursing. *Ravaged* was the word my chest sang like an epic simile where a beaten donkey keeps destroying crops while the bloodshed rages on. Not only because of the baby's tongue tie it took three lactation consultants to notice, but also, they all agreed, because of his mother's nipples. My ex used to tease me they were tiny. Platitudes, not obelisks. He'd touch them, we'd tussle, I'd protest my greatness. I almost called him—*Hey, guess what I need*—when I was given a small piece of silicone called a nipple shield. It protected my skin and gave the baby more bulk to suck. *Where is the epic poem of childbirth?* my friend Ruth has wondered, and just yesterday I heard Madeline Miller ask the same. To help myself heal I also purchased breast shells, which sounded like something an ocean nymph might wear. *Ah me, my sorrow, the bitterness in this best of childbearing.* Thetis is, remember, immortal. I imagine her gliding onto the plain of war to say what no extant epic would have wanted her to say: *Put that down, right now.* And in reply I hear Robert Moses in 1950s New York yelling at Jane Jacobs and her opposition to his plan to build a highway through Greenwich Village: *There is nobody against this—NOBODY, NOBODY, NOBODY, but a bunch of, a bunch of MOTHERS!* I'd lick the nipple shield and stick it on and soon I didn't need it. I'd think of Thetis nursing her gleaming son, a milk-drunk bundle, and her hair floating in the underwater breeze. After all, I am a mammal. This is how I work. How he increases. How I battle my imperfection, his mortality.

On His Beauty

His hair smells like a meadow nobody owns

His seed-sized fingernails
leave scratch marks on my chest
spelling out the name he had before
I delivered him into time

His eyes predict every color of the future except their own

I have seen the shadow of a sparrow fly
over his head asleep in the afternoon
so I have seen the world

I nurse him through the night and at dawn
I eat potato chips

where the wolf tree nurses

in David's Bridal you spread out like a canopy
in the bridesmaid's dress when its alterations needed altered
in front of platformed mirrors you held him
waiting for a seamstress with pins
in her lips, and stood a forest, multiplied, a portent
in plum for every swan-necked bride

in the 1760s farmhouse at the Henry Ford, the busty high-collared housewife
in a family of reenactors told you to use the parlor and almost
instantly a tour filled the room and started snapping pictures as
if you and he and all your leaves were part of the exhibit

in the DIA's café you sat near the only piece of art the museum
invites visitors to touch, a bronze donkey; you
imagined him carrying a clear-eyed man
into an ancient small town waving palm fronds

driving home from the wedding you parked and carried him
into an untended lot of land across from a quarry, empty,
unmanned that Sunday
in the huge shade of a gnarled oak by the banks of the Little Tymochthee Creek
ants and acorns bit your legs
in the grass down the street from a corner market and bar where the walls
enclosing its back patio are made
entirely of old doors old openings their colors peeling away
in strips; it's one way to build a wall

in your pew during Mass when he was quiet and the latch was easy
leaving Mass when he was fussy and it was hard

in the Gethsemane shrine where three
three-dimensional disciples drowse on fake rocks
reclined against painted foothills of cedars and olive trees
in the parish hall, mostly empty during services, you sat once
nursing and talking with a prostitute who came
in for the coffee and donuts; she said her grandchildren lived
far away, she smiled at him

it was dark, that same room
one Holy Thursday, the early
evening rites you had to leave just as the priest began
washing twelve men's feet, the Mass that
ends with all the linens folded and lights turned off toward the agony
in the garden   everyone sits quiet
in the dark before they leave
in a kind of ceremony that refuses itself you carried him crying
into the hall the security guard unlocked
it for you his gun
in a holster on his belt as always
it was dark and filled to overflowing with Easter flowers
in storage for a few days until the stone would roll away
it was you and the boy, and white tables and chairs,
adrift like cottonwood seeds
in the scents—somehow deeper in the dark—of all the blossoms
in this world

Epigraphs on page xi: C. D. Wright, *Casting Deep Shade* (Copper Canyon Press, 2019, p. 166); Stu Sherman, artist essay accompanying photography series *Living With: Self-Portrait of a Diabetic Life* (*Virginia Quarterly Review*, Spring 2020, p. 64); *Iliad* 18.57 (my translation).

"Studies in Devotion" on page 12: Quotes James Wright's poem "A Blessing" and Leonard Cohen's song "Suzanne."

"Coywolf" on page 15: Addresses the new creature described in a 2016 *Newsweek* article, "Enter the Coywolf": "The wolves were remnants, and the coyotes were pioneers. Neither . . . had many choices when it came to finding a mate, and so sometimes the kissing cousins chose each other. The result—along the southern edge of Algonquin Provincial Park around 1920, according to scientists' best estimates—was the formation of a coyote-wolf hybrid."

"Trying," on page 19: References *The Homeric Hymn to Hermes.*

Section vii of "Wolf Trees" on page 36: Quotes Charles Elliott's essay, "Woodman! Spare That 'Wolf' Tree!," published in *American Forests*, Vol. 51, No. 10, 1945.

Section x of "Wolf Trees" on page 39: Quotes Muriel Rukeyser's poem "Islands" and John Donne's "For Whom the Bell Tolls."

"If you secretly wish your child could be secretly baptized," on page 46, is dedicated to the memory of Bob Hart.

"The Nipple Shield of Achilles" on page 82: Quotes *Iliad* 18.54 (Richmond Lattimore's translation) and a 2001 *Metropolis Magazine* interview with Jane Jacobs.

Katie Hartsock is the author of two poetry collections, *Wolf Trees* (2023) and *Bed of Impatiens* (2016), both from Able Muse Press. Her poems appear widely, in journals such as *Ecotone, Poetry, Kenyon Review, 32 Poems*, the *Threepenny Review, Birmingham Poetry Review, Greensboro Review, Pleiades, Dappled Things*, the *New Criterion*, and *Beloit Poetry Journal*. She is an associate professor of English and Creative Writing at Oakland University in Michigan. She lives in Ann Arbor with her husband and their young sons.

ALSO FROM ABLE MUSE PRESS

Jacob M. Appel, *The Cynic in Extremis: Poems*

William Baer, *Times Square and Other Stories; New Jersey Noir: A Novel;*
New Jersey Noir (Cape May): A Novel;
New Jersey Noir (Barnegat Light): A Novel

Lee Harlin Bahan, *A Year of Mourning: Sonnets: (Petrarch) Translation;*
Advent and Lent: Sestinas and Sonnets: (Petrarch) Translation

Melissa Balmain, *Walking in on People (Able Muse Book Award for Poetry)*

Ben Berman, *Strange Borderlands: Poems; Figuring in the Figure: Poems;*
Writing While Parenting: Essays

David Berman, *Progressions of the Mind: Poems*

Lorna Knowles Blake, *Green Hill (Able Muse Book Award for Poetry)*

Michael Cantor, *Life in the Second Circle: Poems*

Catherine Chandler, *Lines of Flight: Poems*

William Conelly, *Uncontested Grounds: Poems*

Maryann Corbett, *Credo for the Checkout Line in Winter: Poems;*
Street View: Poems; In Code: Poems

Will Cordeiro, *Trap Street (Able Muse Book Award for Poetry)*

Brian Culhane, *Remembering Lethe: Poems*

John Philip Drury, *Sea Level Rising: Poems; The Teller's Cage: Poems*

Josh Dugat, *Great and Small: Poems*

Gregory Emilio, *Kitchen Apocrypha: Poems*

Rhina P. Espaillat, *And After All: Poems*

Anna M. Evans, *Under Dark Waters: Surviving the* Titanic: *Poems*

Nicole Caruso Garcia, *Oxblood: Poems*

Stephen Gibson, *Frida Kahlo in Fort Lauderdale: Poems*

Amy Glynn, *Romance Language: Poems*

D. R. Goodman, *Greed: A Confession: Poems*

Carrie Green, *Studies of Familiar Birds: Poems*

Margaret Ann Griffiths, *Grasshopper: The Poetry of M A Griffiths*

Janis Harrington, *How to Cut a Woman in Half: Poems*

Katie Hartsock, *Bed of Impatiens: Poems*

Elise Hempel, *Second Rain: Poems*

Jan D. Hodge, *Taking Shape: Carmina figurata; The Bard & Scheherazade Keep*
Company: Poems; Finesse: Verse and Anagram

Ellen Kaufman, *House Music: Poems; Double-Parked, with Tosca: Poems*

Len Krisak, *Say What You Will (Able Muse Book Award for Poetry)*

Emily Leithauser, *The Borrowed World (Able Muse Book Award for Poetry)*

Hailey Leithauser, *Saint Worm: Poems*

Carol Light, *Heaven from Steam: Poems*

Kate Light, *Character Shoes: Poems*

April Lindner, *This Bed Our Bodies Shaped: Poems*